BODY

Holding one strand **each** of Color A and Color B together, ch 70{74}.

Row 1: Dc in fourth ch from hook **(3 skipped chs count as first dc)** and in each ch across: 68{72} dc.

Row 2: Ch 3 **(counts as first dc)**, turn; dc in next dc and in each dc across.

Repeat Row 2 until Body measures approximately 36{40}"/ 91.5{101.5} cm from beginning ch.

Cut Color A.

EDGING

Rnd 1 (Right side)**:** Holding one strand **each** of Color B and Color C together, ch 1, turn; 3 sc in first dc, sc in each dc across to last dc, 3 sc in last dc; sc evenly across end of rows; working in free loops of beginning ch ***(Fig. 2b, page 22)***, 3 sc in first ch, sc in each ch across to last ch, 3 sc in last ch; sc evenly across end of rows; join with slip st to first sc.

Rnd 2: Ch 1, do **not** turn; sc in each sc around working 3 sc in center sc of each corner 3-sc group; join with slip st to first sc.

Rnd 3: Ch 1, **turn**; sc in each sc around working 3 sc in center sc of each corner 3-sc group; join with slip st to first sc, finish off.

For the most adorable monster play set for little boys or girls, crochet any or all of the easy designs in this book. Two color schemes are shown, but the possibilities are endless. The coordinating hoodie, leggings, and hat are sized for ages 6 months to 4 years. The two blankets are great for creative play or naptime.

LEISURE ARTS, INC. • Maumelle, Arkansas

Furry Blanket

EASY

SHOPPING LIST

Yarn

(Bulky Weight Novelty) BULKY 5

[1.75 ounces, 64 yards
(50 grams, 58 meters) per skein]:

- ☐ Color A (Pink or Blue) - 7{9} skeins

(Medium Weight) MEDIUM 4

[3.5 ounces, 170 yards
(100 grams, 156 meters) per skein]:

- ☐ **Girl Only:** Color B (Dark Pink) - 4 skeins
- ☐ **Boy Only:** Color C (Blue) - 1 skein

[3 ounces, 185 yards
(85 grams, 170 meters) per skein]:

- ☐ **Girl Only:** Color C (Pink) - 1 skein
- ☐ **Boy Only:** Color B (Dark Blue) - 4 skeins

Crochet Hook

- ☐ Size L (8 mm) **or** size needed for gauge

SIZE INFORMATION

Size	Finished Measurement
Small	36" x 38" (91.5 cm x 96.5 cm)
Medium	38" x 42" (96.5 cm x 106.5 cm)

Size Note: We have printed the instructions for the sizes in different colors to make it easier for you to find:

- Size Small in Blue
- Size Medium in Pink

Instructions in Black apply to both sizes.

GAUGE INFORMATION

Holding two strands together,
8 dc = 4" (10 cm),
6 rows = 5½" (14 cm)

Gauge Swatch: 4" wide x 5½" high
(10 cm x 14 cm)

Holding one strand **each** of Color A and Color B together, ch 10.

Row 1: Dc in fourth ch from hook **(3 skipped chs count as first dc)** and in each ch across: 8 dc.

Rows 2-6: Ch 3 **(counts as first dc)**, turn; dc in next dc and in each dc across. Finish off.

The blanket is worked holding two strands of yarn together throughout.

Furry Hoodie

EASY

Instructions begin on page 6.

SHOPPING LIST

Yarn

(Bulky Weight Novelty) BULKY 5
[1.75 ounces, 64 yards
(50 grams, 58 meters) per skein]:

☐ Color A (Pink or Blue) -
{2-3}{3-3-4} skeins

(Medium Weight) MEDIUM 4
[3.5 ounces, 170 yards
(100 grams, 156 meters) per skein]:

☐ **Girl Only:** Color B (Dark Pink) -
{2-2}{2-2-3} skeins

☐ **Boy Only:** Color C (Blue) -
1 skein

[3 ounces, 185 yards
(85 grams, 170 meters) per skein]:

☐ **Girl Only:** Color C (Pink) - 1 skein

☐ **Boy Only:** Color B (Dark Blue) -
{2-2}{2-2-3} skeins

Crochet Hook

☐ Size L (8 mm)
or size needed for gauge

Additional Supplies

☐ Yarn needle

☐ Sewing needle and thread

☐ Zipper - {14-16}{18-20-22}"/
{35.5-40.5}{45.5-51-56} cm length

SIZE INFORMATION

Size	Finished Chest Measurement
6 months	23½" (59.5 cm)
1 year	25½" (65 cm)
2 years	27½" (70 cm)
3 years	29½" (75 cm)
4 years	31½" (80 cm)

Size Note: We have printed the instructions for the sizes in different colors to make it easier for you to find:
- Size 6 months in Blue
- Size 1 year in Pink
- Size 2 years in Green
- Size 3 years in Orange
- Size 4 years in Brown

Instructions in Black apply to all sizes.

GAUGE INFORMATION

Holding two strands together,
8 dc = 4" (10 cm),
6 rows = 5½" (14 cm)

Gauge Swatch: 4" wide x 5½" high
(10 cm x 14 cm)

Holding one strand **each** of Color A and Color B together, ch 10.

Row 1: Dc in fourth ch from hook **(3 skipped chs count as first dc)** and in each ch across: 8 dc.

Rows 2-6: Ch 3 **(counts as first dc)**, turn; dc in next dc and in each dc across.

Finish off.

The hoodie is worked holding two strands of yarn together throughout.

BODY

Body is worked in one piece to armholes, then divided for the Front and Backs.

Holding one strand **each** of Color A and Color B together, ch {46-50}{54-58-62}.

Row 1 (Right side)**:** Dc in fourth ch from hook (**3 skipped chs count as first dc, now and throughout**) and in each ch across: {44-48}{52-56-60} dc.

Note: Loop a short piece of yarn around any stitch to mark Row 1 as **right** side.

Rows 2 thru {6-6}{7-7-8}: Ch 3 (**counts as first dc, now and throughout**), turn; dc in next dc and in each dc across.

FIRST BACK

Row 1: Ch 3, turn; dc in next {10-11}{12-13-14} dc; leave remaining dc unworked: {11-12}{13-14-15} dc.

Rows 2 thru {4-5}{5-6-6}: Ch 3, turn; dc in next dc and in each dc across.

Last Row: Ch 1, turn; sc in each dc across; finish off.

FRONT

Row 1: Join yarn with dc in next unworked dc on Body ***(see Joining With Dc, page 22)***; dc in next {21-23}{25-27-29} dc, leave remaining dc unworked: {22-24}{26-28-30} dc.

Rows 2 thru {3-4}{4-5-5}: Ch 3, turn; dc in next dc and in each dc across.

FIRST SHOULDER

Row 1: Ch 3, turn; dc in next {4-5}{6-7-8} dc, leave remaining dc unworked: {5-6}{7-8-9} dc.

Row 2: Ch 1, turn; sc in each dc across; finish off leaving a long end for sewing.

SECOND SHOULDER

Row 1: Skip next 12 dc from First Shoulder and join yarn with dc in next dc; dc in next dc and in each dc across: {5-6}{7-8-9} dc.

Row 2: Ch 1, turn; sc in each dc across; finish off leaving a long end for sewing.

SECOND BACK

Row 1: Join yarn with dc in next unworked dc on Body; dc in next dc and in each dc across: {11-12}{13-14-15} dc.

Rows 2 thru {4-5}{5-6-6}: Ch 3, turn; dc in next dc and in each dc across.

Last Row: Ch 1, turn; sc in each dc across; finish off.

SLEEVE (Make 2)

Holding one strand **each** of Color A and Color B together, ch {16-16}{17-18-19}.

Row 1 (Right side)**:** Dc in fourth ch from hook and in each ch across: {14-14}{15-16-17} dc.

Note: Mark Row 1 as **right** side.

Row 2 (Increase row)**:** Ch 3, turn; dc in first dc and in each dc across to last dc, 2 dc in last dc: {16-16}{17-18-19} dc.

Repeat Row 2, {0-1}{1-1-1} time(s) ***(see Zeros, page 22)***: {18}{19-20-21} dc.

Work even for {3-3}{4-5-6} rows; finish off leaving a long end for sewing.

HOOD

Holding one strand **each** of Color A and Color B together, ch {32-37}{39-42-45}.

Row 1 (Right side)**:** Dc in fourth ch from hook and in each ch across: {30-35}{37-40-43} dc.

Note: Mark Row 1 as **right** side.

Rows 2 thru {6-7}{8-9-10}: Ch 3, turn; dc in next dc and in each dc across.

Finish off.

HOOD EDGING

Row 1: With **right** side facing, working in free loops of beginning ch *(Fig. 2b, page 22)*, and holding one strand **each** of Color B and Color C together, join yarn with sc in first ch *(see Joining With Sc, page 22)*; sc in each ch across: {30-35}{37-40-43} sc.

Row 2: Ch 1, turn; sc in each sc across; finish off.

FINISHING

With **wrong** sides together, whipstitch shoulder seams *(Fig. 4a, page 23)*.

Sew Sleeves to armholes, matching center of Sleeves to shoulder seams. Whipstitch underarm seam *(Fig. 4b, page 23)*.

SLEEVE CUFF

Rnd 1: With **right** side facing, working in free loops of beginning ch, and holding one strand **each** of Color B and Color C together, join yarn with sc in first ch; sc in each ch around; join with slip st to first sc: {14-14}{15-16-17} sc.

Rnd 2: Ch 1, turn; sc in each sc around; join with slip st to first sc, finish off.

BODY EDGING

Rnd 1: With **right** side facing, working in free loops of beginning ch, and holding one strand **each** of Color B and Color C together, join yarn with sc in first ch on Back; sc in each ch across bottom edge, 3 sc in corner, sc evenly across end of rows; with **right** side of Hood facing, sc in each dc across last row; sc evenly across end of rows on Back; 3 sc in corner; join with slip st to first sc.

Rnd 2: Ch 1, turn; sc in each sc around working 3 sc in each corner sc; join with slip st to first sc, finish off.

Placing each end of Row 2 of Hood Edging together at center Front, sew end of rows to Body.

Sew zipper in place to Back opening.

Little Monster Blanket

EASY

Finished Measurement: 36" wide x 42" long (91.5 cm x 106.5 cm)

SHOPPING LIST

Yarn

(Bulky Weight Novelty) BULKY 5
[1.75 ounces, 64 yards
(50 grams, 58 meters) per skein**]**:

☐ Color A (Pink or Blue) - 4 skeins

(Medium Weight) MEDIUM 4
[3.5 ounces, 170 yards
(100 grams, 156 meters) per skein**]**:

☐ White - 60 yards (55 meters)

☐ Color D (Purple or Red) - 4 skeins

☐ **Girl Only:** Color B (Dark Pink) - 4 skeins

☐ **Boy Only:** Color C (Blue) - 4 skeins

[3 ounces, 185 yards
(85 grams, 170 meters) per skein**]**:

☐ **Girl Only:** Color C (Pink) - 3 skeins

☐ **Boy Only:** Color B (Dark Blue) - 3 skeins

Crochet Hook

☐ Size L (8 mm) **or** size needed for gauge

Additional Supplies

☐ Yarn needle

GAUGE INFORMATION

Holding two strands together,
8 sc and 9 rows = 4" (10 cm)

Gauge Swatch: 4" (10 cm) square
Holding one strand **each** of Color A and Color B together, ch 9.

Row 1: Sc in second ch from hook and in each ch across: 8 sc.

Rows 2-9: Ch 1, turn; sc in each sc across. Finish off.

The blanket is worked holding two strands of yarn together throughout.

TOP TOOTH (Make 12)

Holding two strands of White together, ch 4.

Row 1 (Right side)**:** Sc in second ch from hook and in each ch across: 3 sc.

Note: Loop a short piece of yarn around any stitch to mark Row 1 as **right** side.

Rows 2 and 3: Ch 1, turn; sc in each sc across.

Row 4: Ch 1, turn; pull up a loop in first 3 sc, YO and draw through all 4 loops on hook.

Row 5: Ch 1, turn; sc in st; finish off leaving a long end for sewing.

BODY

Holding one strand **each** of Color B and Color C together, ch 69.

Row 1 (Right side)**:** Sc in second ch from hook and in each ch across: 68 sc.

Note: Mark Row 1 as **right** side.

Row 2: Ch 1, turn; sc in each sc across changing to one strand **each** of Color A and Color B in last sc *(Fig. 3a, page 22)*; do **not** cut yarn.

Row 3: Ch 1, turn; sc in each sc across.

Row 4: Ch 1, turn; sc in each sc across changing to one strand **each** of Color B and Color C in last sc; do **not** cut unused color.

Row 5: Ch 1, turn; sc in each sc across.

Rows 6-17: Repeat Rows 2-5, 3 times.

Row 18: Ch 1, turn; sc in each sc across; cut yarns, finish off.

Row 19: With **right** side facing and holding two strands of Color D together, join yarn with sc in first sc *(see Joining With Sc, page 22)*; sc in next 5 sc, ★ † sc in Back Loop Only of next 3 sc (for Bottom Tooth) *(Fig. 1, page 22)*, sc in **both** loops of next 4 sc, sc in Back Loop Only of next 3 sc †, sc in **both** loops of next 13 sc; repeat from ★ once **more**, then repeat from † to † once, sc in last 6 sc.

Rows 20-36: Ch 1, turn; sc in each sc across; at end of Row 36, finish off.

Row 37: With **right** side facing and holding one strand **each** of Color B and Color C together, join yarn with sc in first sc; sc in next 6 sc, ★ † holding Top Tooth in **front** of work, (sc in free loop of beginning ch on Tooth **and** in next sc) 3 times *(Fig. 2b, page 22)* †, sc in next 2 sc, repeat from † to † once, sc in next 15 sc; repeat from ★ once **more**, then repeat from † to † once, sc in next 2 sc, repeat from † to † once, sc in last 7 sc.

Rows 38-89: Repeat Rows 2-37 once, then repeat Rows 2-17 once **more**.

Row 90: Ch 1, turn; sc in each sc across changing to one strand **each** of Color A and Color B in last sc; cut Color C.

EDGING

Rnd 1: Ch 1, turn; 3 sc in first sc, sc in each sc across to last sc, 3 sc in last sc; sc evenly across end of rows; working in free loops of beginning ch, 3 sc in first ch, sc in each ch across to last ch, 3 sc in last ch; sc evenly across end of rows; drop yarn, holding two strands of Color D together, join with slip st to first sc *(Fig. 3b, page 22)*.

Rnd 2: Ch 1, do **not** turn; sc in each sc around working 3 sc in center sc of each corner 3-sc group; cut Color D, holding one strand each of Color A and Color B together, join with slip st to first sc.

Rnd 3: Ch 1, **turn**; sc in each sc around working 3 sc in center sc of each corner 3-sc group; join with slip st to first sc, finish off.

BOTTOM TOOTH

Row 1: With **right** side facing, holding two strands of White together, and working in free loops of sc on Row 18 *(Fig. 2a, page 22)*, join yarn with sc in first sc; sc in next 2 sc: 3 sc.

Rows 2 and 3: Ch 1, turn; sc in each sc across.

Row 4: Ch 1, turn; pull up a loop in first 3 sc, YO and draw through all 4 loops on hook.

Row 5: Ch 1, turn; sc in st; finish off leaving a long end for sewing.

Repeat for each Bottom Tooth.

Sew all Teeth in place.

Little Monster Hat & Leggings

EASY

SHOPPING LIST

Yarn (Medium Weight) MEDIUM 4

[3 ounces, 185 yards
(85 grams, 170 meters) per skein**]**:

- ☐ Color A (Pink or Dark Blue) - {1-1}{2-2-2} skein(s)

[3.5 ounces, 170 yards
(100 grams, 156 meters) per skein**]**:

- ☐ Color B (Dark Pink or Blue) - {1-1}{2-2-2} skein(s)
- ☐ Color C (Purple or Red) - 1 skein
- ☐ White - small amount
- ☐ Black - small amount

Crochet Hook

- ☐ Size J (6 mm) **or** size needed for gauge

Additional Supplies

- ☐ Yarn needle
- ☐ Sewing needle and thread
- ☐ ¾" (19 mm) wide Elastic (for Leggings)

SIZE INFORMATION

HAT

Size	Finished Circumference
Small	14½" (37 cm)
Medium	16" (40.5 cm)
Large	17¾" (45 cm)

Size Note: We have printed the instructions for the sizes in different colors to make it easier for you to find:

- Size small in Blue
- Size medium in Green
- Size large in Brown

Instructions in Black apply to all sizes.

LEGGINGS

Size	Finished Waist Measurement
6 months	19" (48.5 cm)
1 year	21¾" (55 cm)
2 years	24¾" (63 cm)
3 years	26" (66 cm)
4 years	29" (73.5 cm)

Size Note: We have printed the instructions for the sizes in different colors to make it easier for you to find:

- Size 6 months in Blue
- Size 1 year in Pink
- Size 2 years in Green
- Size 3 years in Orange
- Size 4 years in Brown

Instructions in Black apply to all sizes.

GAUGE INFORMATION

Single strand,
11 sc = 4" (10 cm),
10 rows = 3" (7.5 cm)

Gauge Swatch: 4" wide x 3" high (10 cm x 7.5 cm)

Ch 12.

Row 1: Sc in second ch from hook and in each ch across: 11 sc.

Rows 2-10: Ch 1, turn; sc in each sc across.

Finish off.

STITCH GUIDE

SINGLE CROCHET 2 TOGETHER *(abbreviated sc2tog)*
Pull up a loop in each of next 2 sc, YO and draw through all 3 loops on hook **(counts as one sc)**.

The hat and leggings are worked with a single strand of yarn throughout.

HAT

TOP TOOTH (Make 2)
With White, ch 3.

Row 1: Sc in second ch from hook and in next ch: 2 sc.

Row 2: Ch 1, turn; sc2tog.

Row 3: Ch 1, turn; sc in sc; finish off leaving a long end for sewing.

RIBBING

With Color A and leaving a long end for sewing, ch 7.

Row 1: Sc in second ch from hook and in each ch across: 6 sc.

Rows 2 thru 40{44-49}: Ch 1, turn; sc in Back Loop Only of each sc across ***(Fig. 1, page 22)***.

BODY

Begin working in rounds.

Rnd 1 (Right side)**:** Ch 1, do **not** turn; sc in end of each row across; join with slip st to first sc: 40{44-49} sc.

Note: Loop a short piece of yarn around any stitch to mark Rnd 1 as **right** side.

Rnd 2: Ch 1, turn; sc in each sc around; cut Color A, with Color B, join with slip st to first sc ***(Fig. 3b, page 22)***.

Rnd 3: Ch 1, turn; sc in each sc around; join with slip st to first sc.

Rnd 4: Ch 1, turn; sc in each sc around; cut Color B, with Color C, join with slip st to first sc.

Rnd 5: Ch 1, turn; sc in same st as joining and in next 14{16-18} sc, sc in Back Loop Only of next 3 sc (for Bottom Tooth), sc in **both** loops of next 4{4-5} sc, sc in Back Loop Only of next 3 sc, sc in **both** loops of each sc around; join with slip st to first sc.

Rnds 6 thru 10{12-14}: Ch 1, turn; sc in each sc around; join with slip st to first sc.

Finish off.

SHAPING

Rnd 1: With **right** side of Body facing, join Color B with sc in same st as joining ***(see Joining With Sc, page 22)***; sc in next 16{18-20} sc, † holding Top Tooth in **front** of work, (sc in free loop of beginning ch on Tooth **and** in next sc) twice ***(Fig. 2b, page 22)*** †, sc in next 2{2-3} sc, repeat from † to † once, sc in each sc around; join with slip st to first sc.

Sizes Small & Medium Only - Rnd 2: Ch 1, turn; sc in each sc around; drop Color B, with Color A, join with slip st to first sc, do **not** cut yarn.

Size Large Only - Rnd 2: Ch 1, turn; sc in each sc around to last 2 sc, sc2tog; drop Color B, with Color A, join with slip st to first sc: 48 sc.

All Sizes - Rnd 3: Ch 1, turn; sc in same st as joining and in next sc, sc2tog, (sc in next 2 sc, sc2tog) around; join with slip st to first sc: 30{33-36} sc.

Rnd 4: Ch 1, turn; sc in each sc around; drop Color A, with Color B, join with slip st to first sc.

Rnd 5: Ch 1, turn; sc in same st as joining, sc2tog, (sc in next sc, sc2tog) around; join with slip st to first sc: 20{22-24} sc.

Rnd 6: Ch 1, turn; sc in each sc around; cut Color B, with Color A, join with slip st to first sc.

Rnd 7: Ch 1, turn; beginning in same st as joining, sc2tog around; join with slip st to first sc: 10{11-12} sc.

Rnd 8: Ch 1, turn; beginning in same st as joining, sc2tog around to last 0{1-0} sc, sc in last 0{1-0} sc ***(see Zeros, page 22)***; join with slip st to first sc, finish off: 5{6-6} sc.

BOTTOM TOOTH

Row 1: With **right** side facing and working in free loops of sc on Rnd 4 of Body ***(Fig. 2a, page 22)***, join White with sc in first sc; sc in next 2 sc: 3 sc.

Row 2: Ch 1, turn; pull up a loop in first 3 sc, YO and draw through all 4 loops on hook.

Row 3: Ch 1, turn; sc in st; finish off leaving a long end for sewing.

Repeat for second Bottom Tooth.

Sew all Teeth in place.

EYE (Make 2)

With Black, ch 3; join with slip st to form a ring.

Rnd 1 (Right side)**:** Ch 1, 8 sc in ring; join with slip st to first sc, finish off.

Note: Mark Rnd 1 as **right** side.

Rnd 2: With **right** side facing, join White with sc in same st as joining; sc in same st, 2 sc in each sc around; join with slip st to first sc, finish off leaving a long end for sewing: 16 sc.

Whipstitch Ribbing seam ***(Fig. 4a, page 23)***.

Using photo as a guide for placement, sew Eyes to Shaping.

LEGGINGS

LEFT LEG

TOP TOOTH

With White, ch 4.

Row 1: Sc in second ch from hook and in next 2 chs: 3 sc.

Row 2: Ch 1, turn; pull up a loop in first 3 sc, YO and draw through all 4 loops on hook.

Row 3: Ch 1, turn; sc in st; finish off leaving a long end for sewing.

RIBBING

With Color A and leaving a long end for sewing, ch 7.

Row 1: Sc in second ch from hook and in each ch across: 6 sc.

Rows 2 thru {18-22}{26-28-30}: Ch 1, turn; sc in Back Loop Only of each sc across *(Fig. 1, page 22)*.

BODY

Row 1 (Right side)**:** Ch 1, turn; sc in end of each row across: {18-22}{26-28-30} sc.

Note: Loop a short piece of yarn around any stitch to mark Row 1 as **right** side.

Row 2: Ch 1, turn; sc in each sc across changing to Color B in last sc *(Fig. 3a, page 22)*, do **not** cut yarn.

Carry unused yarn loosely along edge.

Row 3 (Increase row)**:** Ch 1, turn; 2 sc in first sc, sc in each sc across to last sc, 2 sc in last sc: {20-24}{28-30-32} sc.

Row 4: Ch 1, turn; sc in each sc across changing colors in last sc.

Rows 5 thru {20-20}{20-22-24}: Repeat Rows 3 and 4, {8-8}{8-9-10} times: {36-40}{44-48-52} sc.

Next {0-4}{8-8-8} Rows: Work even maintaining color sequence *(see Zeros, page 22)*.

Cut both colors, finish off.

SHAPING

Maintain established color sequence.

Row 1: With **right** side facing, skip first {4-4}{4-5-5} sc and join yarn with sc in next sc *(see Joining With Sc, page 22)*; sc in each sc across to last {4-4}{4-5-5} sc, leave remaining sc unworked: {28-32}{36-38-42} sc.

Row 2: Ch 1, turn; sc in each sc across changing colors in last sc, cut yarn.

Row 3: Ch 1, turn; beginning in first sc, sc2tog, sc in each sc across to last 2 sc, sc2tog: {26-30}{34-36-40} sc.

Row 4: Ch 1, turn; sc in each sc across changing to Color C for mouth; cut yarn.

Mouth is worked in short rows.

Row 5: Ch 1, turn; sc in first {5-5}{5-6-6} sc, sc in Back Loop Only of next 3 sc (for Bottom Tooth), sc in **both** loops of next {5-7}{9-9-11} sc, leave remaining sc unworked: {13-15}{17-18-20} sc.

Row 6: Ch 1, turn; sc in each sc across.

Row 7: Ch 1, turn; sc in each sc across Row 6, sc in next sc on Row 4: {14-16}{18-19-21} sc.

Row 8: Ch 1, turn; sc in each sc across.

Row 9: Ch 1, turn; sc in each sc across Row 8, sc in next sc on Row 4: {15-17}{19-20-22} sc.

Row 10: Ch 1, turn; sc in each sc across changing to same color as Rows 3 and 4 in last sc; cut Color C.

Row 11: Ch 1, turn; sc in first {2-2}{3-3-3} sc, holding Tooth in **front** of work, (sc in free loop of beginning ch on Tooth **and** in next sc) 3 times *(Fig. 2b, page 22)*, sc in **both** loops of each sc across Row 10, sc in next sc on Row 4: {16-18}{20-21-23} sc.

Row 12: Ch 1, turn; sc in each sc across changing colors in last sc resuming color sequence of Body.

Row 13: Ch 1, turn; sc in each sc across Row 12 and Row 4: {26-30}{34-36-40} sc.

Work even maintaining color sequence for {9-9}{11-13-13} rows.

Waist Band: Work even in one color for 10 rows; at end of last row, finish off.

BOTTOM TOOTH

Row 1: With **right** side facing and working in free loops of sc on Row 4 *(Fig. 2a, page 22)*, join White with sc in first sc; sc in next 2 sc: 3 sc.

Row 2: Ch 1, turn; sc in each sc across.

Row 3: Ch 1, turn; pull up a loop in first 3 sc, YO and draw through all 4 loops on hook.

Row 4: Ch 1, turn; sc in st; finish off leaving a long end for sewing.

Sew both Teeth in place.

RIGHT LEG

Work same as Left Leg through Row 3 of Shaping.

Row 4: Ch 1, turn; sc in each sc across; cut both colors, finish off.

Mouth is worked in short rows.

Row 5: With **right** side facing, skip first {13-15}{17-18-20} sc and join Color C with sc in next sc; sc in next {4-6}{8-8-10} sc, sc in Back Loop Only of next 3 sc (for Bottom Tooth), sc in **both** loops of each sc across: {13-15}{17-18-20} sc.

Row 6: Ch 1, turn; sc in each sc across Row 5, sc in next sc on Row 4: {14-16}{18-19-21} sc.

Row 7: Ch 1, turn; sc in each sc across.

Row 8: Ch 1, turn; sc in each sc across Row 7, sc in next sc on Row 4: {15-17}{19-20-22} sc.

Row 9: Ch 1, turn; sc in each sc across.

Row 10: Ch 1, turn; sc in each sc across Row 9 changing to same color as Rows 3 and 4 in last sc; cut Color C, sc in next sc on Row 4: {16-18}{20-21-23} sc.

Row 11: Ch 1, turn; sc in first {11-13}{14-15-17} sc, holding Tooth in **front** of work, (sc in free loop of beginning ch on Tooth **and** in next sc) 3 times, sc in **both** loops of each sc across.

Row 12: Ch 1, turn; sc in each sc across Row 11; finish off.

Row 13: With **right** side facing and resuming color sequence of Body, join yarn with sc in first sc on Row 4; sc in each sc across Row 4 and Row 12: {26-30}{34-36-40} sc.

Complete same as Left Leg.

ASSEMBLY

Whipstitch Shaping of both Legs together ***(Figs. 4a & b, page 23)***. Whipstitch inner leg seam.

Fold Waistband in half to **wrong** side and sew in place, leaving an opening for the elastic. Insert the elastic in the Waistband casing. Adjust the elastic to fit your child, overlapping the ends 1" (2.5 cm). Sew ends of elastic together. Finish sewing Waistband in place.

General Instructions

ABBREVIATIONS

ch(s)	chain(s)
cm	centimeters
dc	double crochet(s)
mm	millimeters
Rnd(s)	Round(s)
sc	single crochet(s)
sc2tog	single crochet 2 together
st(s)	stitch(es)
YO	yarn over

SYMBOLS & TERMS

★ — work instructions following ★ as many **more** times as indicated in addition to the first time.

† to † — work all instructions from first † to second † **as many** times as specified.

( ) or [ ] — work enclosed instructions **as many** times as specified by the number immediately following **or** work all enclosed instructions in the stitch or space indicated **or** contains explanatory remarks.

colon (:) — the number(s) given after a colon at the end of a row or round denote(s) the number of stitches or spaces you should have on that row or round.

work even — work without increasing or decreasing in the established pattern.

Yarn Weight Symbol & Names	LACE 0	SUPER FINE 1	FINE 2	LIGHT 3	MEDIUM 4	BULKY 5	SUPER BULKY 6	JUMBO 7
Type of Yarns in Category	Fingering, size 10 crochet thread	Sock, Fingering, Baby	Sport, Baby	DK, Light Worsted	Worsted, Afghan, Aran	Chunky, Craft, Rug	Super Bulky, Roving	Jumbo, Roving
Crochet Gauge* Ranges in Single Crochet to 4" (10 cm)	32-42 sts**	21-32 sts	16-20 sts	12-17 sts	11-14 sts	8-11 sts	6-9 sts	5 sts and fewer
Advised Hook Size Range	Steel*** 6 to 8, Regular hook B-1	B-1 to E-4	E-4 to 7	7 to I-9	I-9 to K-10½	K-10½ to M/N-13	M/N-13 to Q	Q and larger

*GUIDELINES ONLY: The chart above reflects the most commonly used gauges and hook sizes for specific yarn categories.

CROCHET TERMINOLOGY		
UNITED STATES		INTERNATIONAL
slip stitch (slip st)	=	single crochet (sc)
single crochet (sc)	=	double crochet (dc)
half double crochet (hdc)	=	half treble crochet (htr)
double crochet (dc)	=	treble crochet (tr)
treble crochet (tr)	=	double treble crochet (dtr)
double treble crochet (dtr)	=	triple treble crochet (ttr)
triple treble crochet (tr tr)	=	quadruple treble crochet (qtr)
skip	=	miss

CROCHET HOOKS																	
U.S.	B-1	C-2	D-3	E-4	F-5	G-6	7	H-8	I-9	J-10	K-10½	L-11	M/N-13	N/P-15	P/Q	Q	S
Metric - mm	2.25	2.75	3.25	3.5	3.75	4	4.5	5	5.5	6	6.5	8	9	10	15	16	19

BEGINNER	Projects for first-time crocheters using basic stitches. Minimal shaping.
EASY	Projects using yarn with basic stitches, repetitive stitch patterns, simple color changes, and simple shaping and finishing.
INTERMEDIATE	Projects using a variety of techniques, such as basic lace patterns or color patterns, mid-level shaping and finishing.
EXPERIENCED	Projects with intricate stitch patterns, techniques and dimension, such as non-repeating patterns, multi-color techniques, fine threads, small hooks, detailed shaping and refined finishing.

GAUGE

Exact gauge is **essential** for proper size or fit. Before beginning your project, make the sample swatch given in the individual instructions in the yarn and hook specified.
After completing the swatch, measure it, counting your stitches and rows carefully. If your swatch is larger or smaller than specified, **make another, changing hook size to get the correct gauge**. Keep trying until you find the size hook that will give you the specified gauge.

ZEROS

To consolidate the length of an involved pattern, Zeros are sometimes used so that all sizes can be combined. For example, sc2tog around to last 0{1-0} sc, sc in last 0{1-0} sc, means the second size would sc2tog around to the last sc, then sc in last sc; the smallest and largest sizes would sc2tog around.

JOINING WITH SC

When instructed to join with sc, begin with a slip knot on hook. Insert hook in stitch or space indicated, YO and pull up a loop, YO and draw through both loops on hook.

JOINING WITH DC

When instructed to join with dc, begin with a slip knot on hook. YO, holding loop on hook, insert hook in stitch or space indicated, YO and pull up a loop (3 loops on hook), (YO and draw through 2 loops on hook) twice.

BACK LOOP ONLY

Work only in loop(s) indicated by arrow *(Fig. 1)*.

Fig. 1

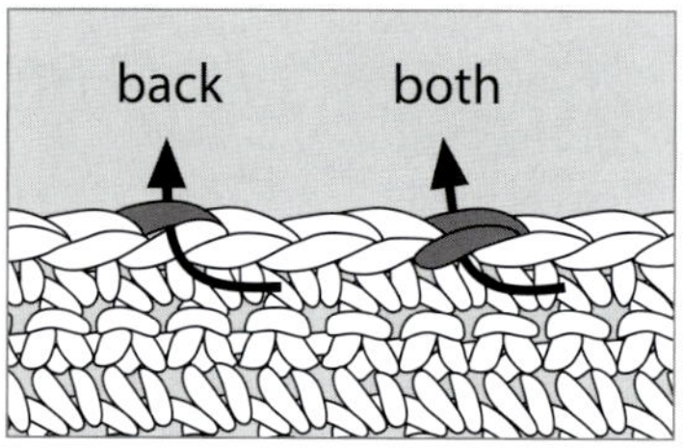

FREE LOOPS

After working in Back Loops Only on a row or round, there will be a ridge of unused loops. These are called the free loops. Later, when instructed to work in the free loops of the same row or round, work in these loops *(Fig. 2a)*.

Fig. 2a

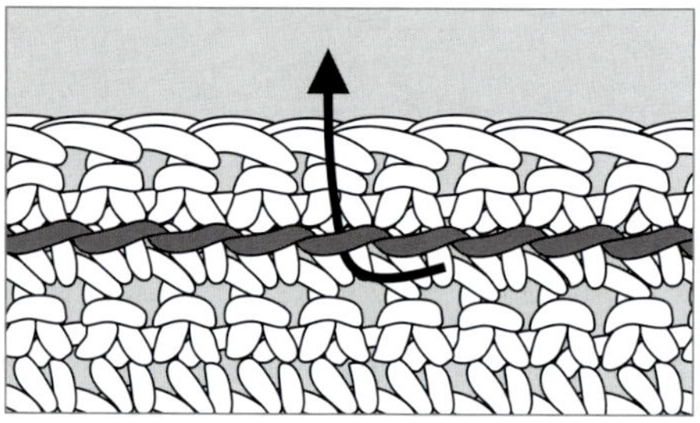

When instructed to work in free loops of a chain, work in loop indicated by arrow *(Fig. 2b)*.

Fig. 2b

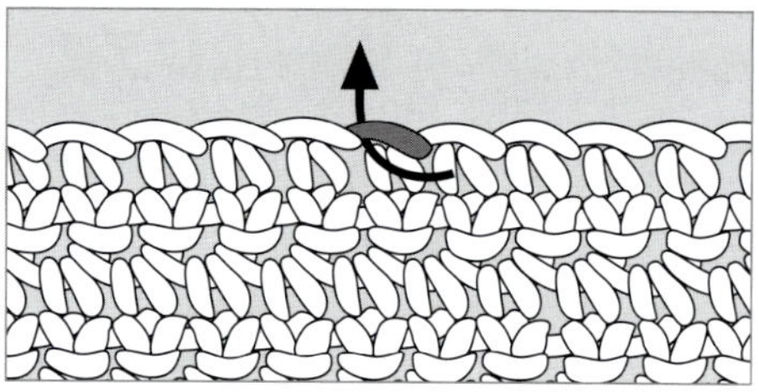

CHANGING COLORS

To change colors while working a sc, insert hook in stitch indicated, YO and pull up a loop, drop yarn, with new yarn *(Fig. 3a)*, YO and draw through both loops on hook.

Fig. 3a

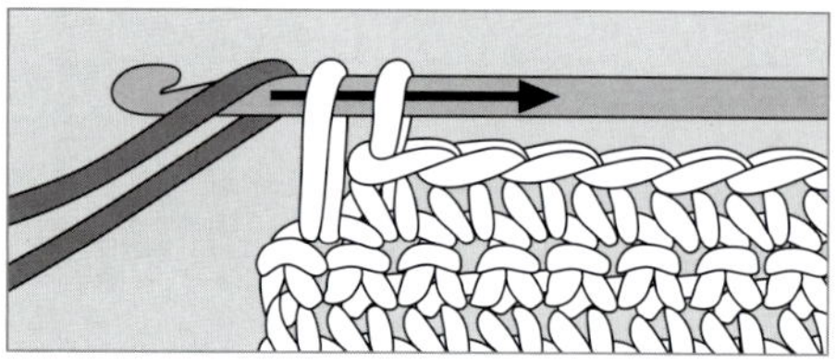

To change colors while joining with a slip st, drop yarn, insert hook in first stitch, hook new yarn and draw through st and loop on hook *(Fig. 3b)*.

Fig. 3b

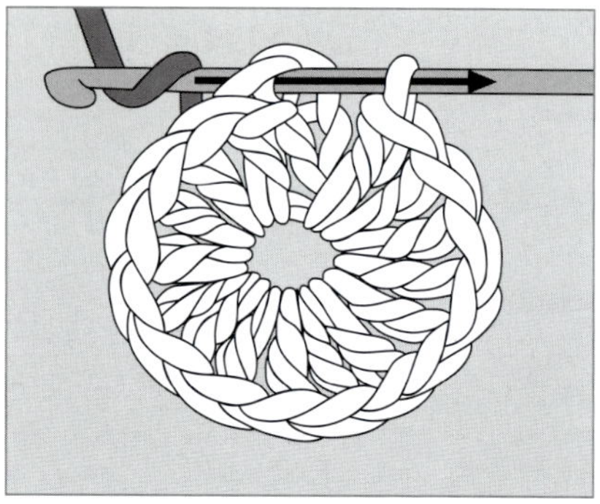

WHIPSTITCH

With **wrong** sides together, sew through both pieces once to secure the beginning of the seam, leaving an ample yarn end to weave in later. Insert the needle from **right** to **left** through two strands on each piece *(Fig. 4a)* **or** through end of rows *(Fig. 4b)*. Bring the needle around and insert it from **right** to **left** through the next strand on both pieces.

Repeat along the edge, being careful to match stitches or rows.

Fig. 4a

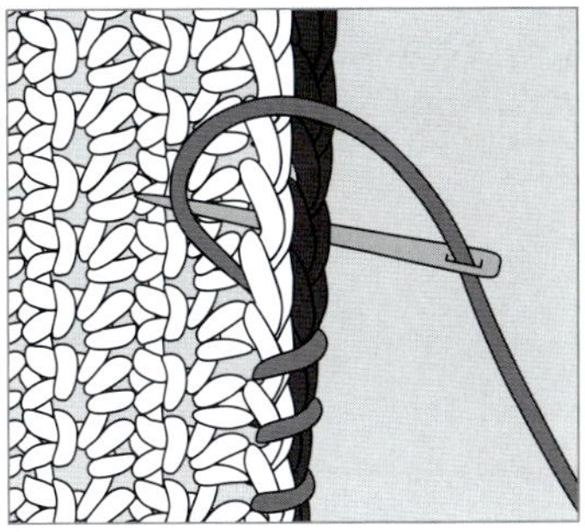

Fig. 4b

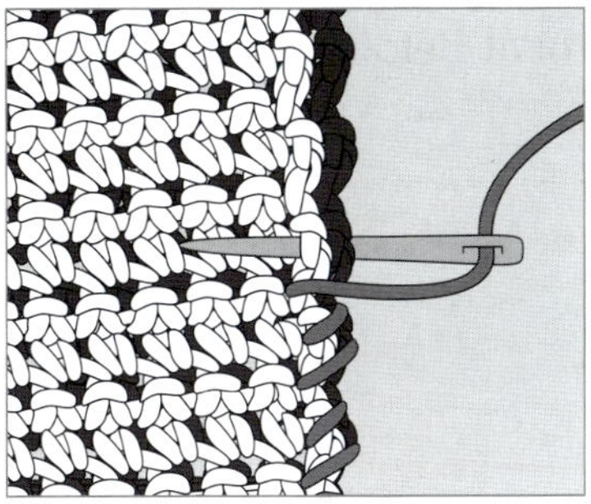

Meet Michele Maks

A crochet and knit designer since 1985, Michele Maks has lost count of the thousands of creations she has made, but she hasn't lost her enthusiasm.

"The next project is always the most exciting!" she says. "I never work on one thing at a time. I'm probably most fascinated by (dare I say it?) granny squares!"

Her designs have appeared in magazines, books, and yarn industry publications.

"Having opinionated children and teaching let me know what worked style-wise and from a stitcher's point of view – both extremely helpful as reality checks!"

A diagnosis of multiple sclerosis in 2009 hasn't stopped her. "Crochet has been a constant solace in battling the effects of this disease," she says.

MainlyCrochet.org, her online subscription service, offers digital patterns for all skill levels. Michele also may be found on Facebook, Ravelry, and mainlycrochetsblog.blogspot.com.

Yarn Information

The items in this book were made using a variety of yarns. Any brand of the specific weight of yarn may be used. It is best to refer to the yardage/meters when determining how many balls or skeins to purchase. Remember, to arrive at the finished size, it is the GAUGE/TENSION that is important, not the brand of yarn.

For your convenience, listed below are the yarns used to create our photography models. Because yarn manufacturers make frequent changes in their product lines, you may sometimes find it necessary to use a substitute yarn or to search for the discontinued product at alternate suppliers (locally or online).

PINK COLOR SCHEME

Lion Brand® Fun Fur®
Pink - #112 Raspberry

Lion Brand® Vanna's Choice®
Dark Pink - #112 Raspberry
Purple - #145 Eggplant
White - #100 White
Black - #153 Black

Lion Brand® Vanna's Complement
Pink - #138 Pink Poodle

BLUE COLOR SCHEME

Lion Brand® Fun Fur®
Blue - #109 Sapphire

Lion Brand® Vanna's Choice® Baby
Blue - #108 Bluebell

Lion Brand® Vanna's Choice®
Red - #113 Scarlet
White - #100 White
Black - #153 Black

Lion Brand® Vanna's Complement
Dark Blue - #109 Colonial Blue

We have made every effort to ensure that these instructions are accurate and complete.
We cannot, however, be responsible for human error, typographical mistakes, or variations in individual work.

Production Team: Instructional/Technical Editor - Cathy Hardy; Editorial Writer - Susan Frantz Wiles;
Senior Graphic Artist - Lora Puls; Graphic Artist - Kellie McAnulty; Photo Stylist - Lori Wenger; and Photographer - Jason Masters.